WHEN SPIRITUALITY AND TRAUMA COLLIDE

WHEN SPIRITUALITY AND TRAUMA COLLIDE

*A Guidebook for
Practitioners of Soul Care*

Karen Bartlett

**invite
PRESS**

Plano, Texas

I would like to dedicate this book to my husband Rick who supported me throughout the writing process and encouraged me to publish, as well as Grace and Tobias, who believed in me as I pursued further education in neuroscience and trauma. I'm grateful for the friends and family who have cheered me on over the past years; none of this would have happened without the backing of those who felt I had something to offer in the realm of spirituality, trauma, and healing. Finally, thank you to Invite Resources for the invaluable help in publishing this handbook.

This book is printed on acid-free, elemental chlorine-free paper.

ISBN 978-1-953495-79-2; ePub 978-1-953495-80-8
All Scripture quotations unless noted otherwise are taken from the New Revised Standard Version of the Bible, copyright 1989, Division of Christian Education of the National Council of the Churches of Christ in the United States of America. Used by permission. All rights reserved.

Scripture quotations marked NIV are taken from THE HOLY BIBLE, NEW INTERNATIONAL VERSION®, NIV® Copyright © 1973, 1978, 1984, 2011 by Biblica, Inc.™ Used by permission of Zondervan. All rights reserved worldwide.

23 24 25 26 27 28 29 30 31 32—10 9 8 7 6 5 4 3 2 1

MANUFACTURED IN THE UNITED STATES OF AMERICA

Table of Contents

Introduction

The practice of spiritual direction has been around since roughly AD 300 but has recently made a resurgence in faith communities and is becoming more popular as people seek spiritual guidance in these uncertain times. The title itself can be confusing or misleading as one might think it means someone will tell you what to do or has more wisdom and insight than the directee (the term for those who are seeing a spiritual director). Yet this is not at all what spiritual direction is, in my opinion. It is the practice of helping others discern what is in their soul, examine belief systems, make space for questions or doubts, and discover their own connection with God and faith by asking questions and creating space to interact with spiritual experiences and move toward inner healing.

In my work as a spiritual director and social worker for more than thirty years, I have encountered an increasing number of individuals working with past or current trauma who are trying to make sense of how faith and trauma can co-exist. The questions revolve around God, faith, evil, pain, childhood abuse, abandonment, religion, biblical promises, and much more. How do all these intersect, especially for those with personal experiences of growing up going to church learning one thing—that God is good and all is well—but being subjected to pain and suffering at home where God seems absent? Did God really care what was going on in those horrible moments? Is faith even relevant when examining trauma? These kinds of questions are deep, painful, confusing, frustrating, honest, and necessary.

My main goal in spiritual direction is to do no harm or further damage to the directee by asking insensitive questions, using traumatizing language, or communicating false narratives that increase shame or guilt.

This handbook developed through my quest to understand how to encounter these soul-searching and sacred conversations with grace, acceptance, honor, and freedom. Part of that quest led me to do a Masters of Neuroscience and Trauma through Tabor College in addition to my post-graduate education in theology from Fresno Pacific Biblical Seminary. I wanted to understand how my learning in social work, theology, and neuroscience could weave together a better approach to spiritual direction for the sake of those who have experienced great harm. When the opportunity arose to do a project for my neuroscience and trauma degree, I jumped at the chance to research best practices from what experts—those who had done this a long time and offer wisdom and experience—had to say about the effects of trauma and how to approach trauma-related issues.

My desire to create this handbook for anyone working with trauma is born out of an awareness that we are seeking to do our best to help others, whether we are spiritual directors, counselors, chaplains, pastors, or in any other capacity that moves others toward wholeness and healing. However, I am fully aware that, personally, I need to constantly learn and grow in understanding how to assist in soul-healing. My hope is that the handbook provides a few more tools to assist those of us who sojourn with others as they move toward wholeness and integration of faith and trauma.

1

When Spirituality and Trauma Collide

A woman came into my office and hesitantly sat down across from me, displaying nervousness and anxiety as her hands twisted in her lap. After a few minutes of general conversation and asking her what brought her to spiritual direction, she haltingly told me that she was evil, unwanted, and abandoned. As her story unfolded, her eyes held the grief and woundedness of trauma from childhood as well as doubt and confusion as to her own sense of being. She began talking about spirituality and God when suddenly her face and body transformed into one of pain and suffering. Her body curled up, and tears coursed down her face, her eyes downcast with shame. With courage and bravery, she told me more details of childhood sexual abuse and wondered where God had been during those horrific moments, as she dealt with the pain of feeling alone and abandoned. She could not come to terms with the internal conflict of trying to believe that God was *good* in the wake of her horrific experiences as a child.

Her story and questions hung in the air as we allowed silence to embrace and hold the sacredness of what she had just shared with me, her spiritual director. My heart was filled with compassion and yet also helplessness. I knew that the one thing I did not want to do was to add to her hurt or confusion, but I was unsure of what to do or say next.

That was years ago. As a spiritual director I am often presented with questions, doubt, confusion, and pain regarding the intersection of faith and childhood abuse or trauma: "How does a loving God let horrible things happen to an innocent child? Where was God when I was being violated and abused? Does God even care that this happened to me? I was taught that God cared, but really?" As I listen to these gut-wrenching and painful questions, they echo in my mind and cause restlessness in my heart. Although I have been a licensed social worker for more than thirty years and have encountered some very dark situations in my career, as a spiritual director I can feel uncertain about how to embrace these kinds of questions about faith and trauma, and sometimes feel at a loss as to how to engage in these conversations without inflicting further damage on a directee.

My own insecurities and uncertainty about handling trauma in the spiritual direction setting move me to read anything I can get my hands on about how to handle trauma and spirituality. Although I found a few good resources, I quickly realized that resources on this topic are scarce or difficult to find. It appears to be an area that is gaining more attention and traction, which is wonderful, and also ignited within me a desire to pursue learning and a passion to gain helpful knowledge for myself, spiritual directors, chaplains, and anyone else who is helping others come to terms with faith and deep inner pain.

Therefore, over the past few years, I have been exploring and researching what is available regarding these sensitive situations of spirituality and trauma and how to manage these difficult and soulful conversations. I have collated what I have learned for the sake of spiritual directors and others who are struggling or need some guidance on spirituality and abuse or trauma.

The information provided in this handbook is an introduction to many of the issues addressed such as trauma, attachment, and neuroscience, and does not comprehensively cover each issue. By definition, trauma is the individual reaction and response to what has happened to someone, not necessarily the event itself. I also do not provide specific spiritual practices or exercises for trauma-related conversations, because each session is unique and requires intentional listening for what might be helpful in the moment. My hope is that you will be inspired to learn more about whatever piques your curiosity as you read this material.

Why Does It Matter?

When someone sits across the room and speaks about the past, that moment becomes sacred. The story itself can be fragile and vulnerable. The information must be handled with respect and gentleness. It cannot be dismissed, addressed with glib words of assurance, or treated as insignificant. Anyone in the role of a spiritual director has the responsibility to be informed and aware of how to interact with directees who have had severe trauma in their past and to make sure we, as spiritual directors, are not inflicting more damage or harm by our questions, conversation, or misinformed guidance.

This handbook investigates how spiritual beliefs about the Christian God, specifically in relation to God as Father/Mother or Protector, can either positively or negatively impact healing memories for someone who has experienced childhood abuse by a caretaker, trusted individual, or within the church. Why? As spiritual healers, we long for an individual to experience transformation and growth over the course of time in spiritual direction, and our hearts seek to be witnesses of healing in those who are hurting or struggling with faith in general. Spiritual direction is all about listening, reflecting, and exploring doubts, questions, concerns, or curiosity about one's faith. Trauma reveals complex layers of questions, doubts, and struggles in the healing journey that require sensitivity and vulnerability.

For myself, encountering more and more individuals with a history of trauma creates an urgency for education and awareness when working with trauma survivors. As I pursued education in neuroscience and trauma, the knowledge of what I learned through study in social work began to make more sense in how the mind, body, and soul connects and affects our entire neurobiological system. The last chapter provides best practices for engaging in spirituality and trauma, gleaned through others' advice and greater understanding of how the mind and body store memories and responses to trauma. In talking with other spiritual directors, I began to realize that they also struggle working with directees who are internally conflicted about the interface of any kind of trauma and faith, particularly regarding the Christian teaching they may have received as children that God protects and is a good Father/Mother but experienced abusive situations. Being called to be a spiritual director is beautiful and fulfilling, yet it can sometimes be a demanding role that weighs heavily on our hearts and minds.

Basic Conflict

The handbook centers on this statement: *The belief in God as Protector or trustworthy Parent often becomes conflictual when attempting to make sense of faith in the wake of childhood trauma.* As a spiritual director, I hear the confusion, pain, and frustration in how a person's experience of childhood trauma impacts faith/beliefs. Often, the person is expressing doubt, confusion, or a desire to understand how their belief in God as Protector or Father/Mother has been impacted by the memories and pain of their childhood trauma, especially sexual abuse. They often experience a disconnect between wanting to believe that God is a good parent and protector and the reality of having been traumatized and/or sexually violated as a child. It does not make sense. They feel severe cognitive and emotional dissonance.

This is an area of extreme importance to me when I am working with individuals to create new, positive, and healing neural pathways of self-worth and value and integration with faith. As the directee and I move toward identifying core beliefs about one's sense of self, the directee often expresses deep conflict around spiritual teachings from childhood and the reality of deep wounding by those who were supposed to be worthy of trust. As a result of these sometimes surprising realizations, hidden doubts about God emerge, and the directee often questions his or her personal worth or value due to the actions or words communicated through the memories of these traumatic events.

It is crucial to understand this inner conflict regarding God and self-worth because the spiritual direction discipline must incorporate an understanding of human nature as it exists in a social, cultural, spiritual, mental, and emotional context. Directors cannot work with individuals and spirituality in a vacuum, separate from other parts of life. Behaviors, beliefs, and values develop from childhood teaching, experiences, and events; therefore, it is essential for a director to continue expanding knowledge about spiritual integration within the whole of a person's life experience, including trauma.

Neuroscience research is opening floodgates of understanding about the complexity of the body/brain interaction. This is critical information for spiritual direction when working with individuals who are shaped and formed by intrinsic and extrinsic forces from pre-birth to the current age. Spiritual directors need to learn not only how spirituality shapes and forms one's sense of self and integration with the world, but also how family dynamics and emotional wounds impact beliefs about the self. Beliefs shape behavior. Research on how the brain receives information and then acts on that information remains an essential component to increasing awareness of the complexity of humanity and how we can reshape and re-form the thinking patterns and belief systems that may have developed through faulty or false childhood narratives.

Reshaping faulty narratives leads to the larger, more complex questions of how spirituality intersects with trauma. How can spirituality be a positive element rather than a barrier in neuroplasticity (creating new neural pathways) for reframing one's story toward wholeness and a healthier sense of self? How does someone make sense of God as Father or Mother when a parent figure may have been abusive? Does faith hinder or help make sense of trauma as a young person or adult? How does faith play a role in restructuring toxic or intrusive thoughts that keep a person prisoner to negative thoughts and/or behavior?

Addressing basic conflicts of faith, childhood narratives, and trauma is key for spiritual directors working with these questions and helping trauma survivors move to a place of mental, spiritual, and emotional healing. New neural networks of belief and behavior are possible, but becoming aware of interactions that could be triggering or insensitive is important for the sake of our directees. When talking with individuals who are grappling with the issues of God as protector, mother, or father, it is imperative to utilize best practices to help a directee work through these incongruent concepts.

2
What Are the Issues?

This chapter explores what might happen within the spiritual direction session and what to be aware of when meeting with a directee who has experienced trauma. We don't always know that a person comes in with a traumatic background, and this is exactly what we must be paying attention to in conversations. Someone might not be ready to overtly tell the director about an abusive past; therefore reading clues is an important aspect of spiritual direction.

I'm Not Sure What I Believe

For a spiritual director, being aware of how an individual processes childhood teachings, beliefs, and understanding of faith in the wake of childhood abuse is critical. In my experience, some people find solace and comfort in their faith when exploring the issue of abuse; others find faith distressing or cannot make sense of God and faith when processing childhood trauma. Another researcher states, "Spirituality can both contribute to resiliency (the ability to bounce back after hardship) and can intensify the pain and distress."[1] We simply do not know how a trauma survivor interprets faith. It could be a source of comfort, or it could be

---

1. Mary Patricia Van Hook, "Spirituality as a potential resource for coping with trauma," *Social Work and Christianity* 43, no. 1 (2016): 12.

a cause of confusion or angst. It can never be assumed that every person sees God as good or faith as a warm, comfy blanket. This type of assumption can be dangerous and is an area of caution for spiritual directors.

Another area of belief that demands sensitivity is the question of *how* spirituality can be part of the recovery journey. Following the directee's lead in discussing spiritual matters and who God is can open the door to conversation about how faith can be part of the healing process. The spiritual director must be curious about the directee's core beliefs and origin of faith for productive dialogue and for discovery of faulty or unhealthy beliefs regarding trauma and spirituality. However, this exploration is effective only if the spiritual director allows the directee to proceed at a tolerable pace of soul excavation, and if the director can contain his/her own beliefs without projecting those onto the client. Maintaining an open mind to what the directee is saying, no matter how much it might conflict with the director's own beliefs, is absolutely key for helping the directee move toward inner healing. Being able to express thoughts, doubts, and questions without judgment allows directees to feel validated and heard as they explore how faith can be part of their healing journey.

Trauma and God as Parent

As stated earlier, understanding how childhood trauma radically affects one's belief of God as parent or protector is essential when working with individuals in a spiritual direction setting. The concept of God as a loving parent can be completely altered when viewed through the lens of abuse, specifically in regard to childhood sexual abuse. Sue Magrath, a mental health therapist and spiritual director, states that an infant who experiences abuse may not remember the abuse; however, in later life, the image of God might emerge subconsciously as a deity who failed to protect a child or is even "capable of the violation of a helpless infant."[2] Being aware of this information impacts sensitivity to conversations centering on abuse and the image of God. Spiritual directors unaware of such depth of pain or wounding may do considerable damage to a directee if the impact of trauma is ignored, dismissed, or unacknowledged regarding personal beliefs about the nature of God. Dismissing someone's concept of God as wrong or immature can reinforce feelings of victimization and/or abuse of authority, therefore being conscious of our response to a directee must be at the forefront of the director's awareness.

Spiritual directors and anyone else who works with people moving toward mental and emotional wholeness need to understand how abuse impacts belief. Images of God created from trauma remain largely unaddressed in the wider spiritual community. For example, in Christian teaching via Sunday school or from the pulpit, God is often presented as a healthy, loving, benevolent, compassionate Father who cares for and protects his children. Or God might be presented as a judgmental, harsh, critical, and demanding Father who *lovingly* disciplines his children with punishment. For children who grow up with either of these teachings and experience abuse by a biological father, it can be confusing, debilitating, puzzling, and chaotic to make sense of who God is and what a healthy relationship with God looks like. Educating the community or spiritual group surrounding survivors of trauma is one way to continue the effort of minimizing further damage to those who are wounded. For starters, we need to be cognizant that words can hurt unintentionally.

2. Sue Magrath, *Healing the Ravaged Soul* (Eugene, OR: Cascade, 2016), 29.

Words Matter

As spiritual directors, we can often use terms with clients that create more trauma, emotional injury, or an unsafe environment due to the failure to recognize the negative effect a word can have on the person sitting across from us. Painting an image of God as Father (or Mother) in relation to a biological parent can present extreme difficulties for individuals who were traumatized in childhood by a parent figure and can create further trauma if not done correctly or with sensitivity. It's like holding up a mirror and wanting the person to see God reflected as good, patient, and kind, but the image the directee sees is one of hate, rejection, or disgust.

Words or phrases are often used in a session without thought as to how they might affect a person who is suffering from traumatic memories: "When young children experience trauma from parents, phrases like 'God is your father, your heavenly father' can create negative and judgmental images of God shaped by the parent. Experiences with parents (both positive and negative) get transferred to their spiritual life."[3] When talking with individuals who are negatively impacted by words about family of origin, this is a signal of distress, and the spiritual director must focus on paying attention to these signals and react with sensitivity. This is further addressed in the next chapter.

For example, referencing the word *Father* or *Daddy* can conjure images of violence, control, coercion, or terror. When discussing sensory input, Perry and Winfrey state that "when children have abusive fathers, their brains begin to connect men with threat, anger, and fear. And this worldview gets built in—men

3. Van Hook, "Spirituality as a potential resource for coping with trauma," 16.

are dangerous, threatening, and will hurt you and the people you love."[4] When talking about God as Father in a session, we may see a visceral response from the client such as the body shuddering or slumping forward, or a facial expression of horror; the individual may shut down, go silent, and withdraw from verbal engagement. Other times there may be no *external* signs of response, but *internal* emotions have been activated that severely affect the directee, who might change tone of voice or sound distant and disengaged. Such an unexpected response may be a surprise for the director, but it signals the need for acute attention in using sensitive and altered verbal language when working with clients who are victims of childhood abuse.

Reading the Cues

When asked about a strong response to a specific term used in a session, a directee may not know what caused the behavior or may not be aware of the reaction. It is important for directors to understand that even when the threat of trauma has been removed, the person may not be able to discern whether he or she is safe in the moment; therefore, they may respond as if re-experiencing the traumatic moment. "Traumatized people chronically feel unsafe inside their bodies: The past is alive in the form of gnawing interior discomfort. Their bodies are constantly bombarded by visceral warning signs . . . they learn to hide from themselves."[5] Regardless of whether someone remembers the traumatic event itself or experiences negative affect without memory recall, the director needs to be keenly aware of a shift in the room

---

4. Bruce Perry and Oprah Winfrey, *What Happened to You?* (New York, NY: Flatiron Books, 2021), 32.

5. Bessel Van der Kolk, *The Body Keeps the Score* (New York, NY: Penguin Books, 2014), 99.

and in the directee and respond accordingly with different language or heightened curiousity.

For example, a free-flowing conversation can suddenly stop and become jerky or awkward at best due to a word or idea that has set off alarm bells for the directee who may not feel personal agency to let the director know he/she does not feel safe or needs to stop the conversation. Therefore, it is imperative that the director gives verbal permission in the initial session for the directee to put a halt to any conversation or spiritual practice at any time without explanation. This action alone can create a place of trust or safety for the directee from the outset and foster deeper conversation regarding one's spiritual beliefs.

The Body Speaks, and We Must Listen

Sometimes we assume that God is automatically trustworthy to a directee, but this may be far from the truth. Trust may be the most significantly damaged element in a faith relationship. "Confidence, trust, commitment, promises—these are all immensely frightening words for someone whose body and spirit have been appallingly violated by their abusers."[6]

Paying attention to how a client inhabits a post-traumatic response is essential for the director-directee relationship to survive and continue. If a director dismisses a strong physical or emotional response to language used during the session, it can impair future sessions and deplete trust from the directee.

Trust is a basic element of human interaction that can be eroded or impacted by abuse in childhood, making it a priority to protect and maintain trust in the healing setting. Recogniz-

---

6.   Magrath, *Healing the Ravaged Soul*, 35.

ing that trust may be difficult to establish can help a director be patient and understanding in building that sense of rapport with a directee. Again, to promote an emotional and healing connection with a directee, it is essential to create a relationship of trust through attunement to the directee's body response to triggering words or phrases: "Traumatized people are often afraid of feeling. It is . . . their own physical sensations that now are the enemy . . . even though the trauma is a thing of the past, the emotional brain keeps generating sensations that make the sufferer feel scared and helpless."[7] We can get impatient or confused when a directee cannot simply name emotions at the drop of a hat, and that may cause us to become anxious or frustrated; but understanding that naming and feeling emotions is a major roadblock from trauma can help us soften our response and move us into a more relaxed posture of waiting.

Another tricky area is wanting a directee to feel God's love and embrace it immediately, and it can be tempting to manipulate that end game. But no matter how desirous a spiritual director might be to help a directee feel something positive toward God or to create an image of a trustworthy Being, it can never be forced. This might be a challenge for directors who have not experienced abuse or trauma and fail to grasp the enormity of what damage any type of coercion can inflict upon the directee. Building trust with the director and with God, as well as maintaining a sense of safety, requires sensitivity and the ethical directive of engaging the directee on his/her terms without imposing self-identified beliefs upon the individual.

The loss of a person's trust in self and humanity, including trust in God, is difficult to restore and can be done only in safe

---

7. Van der Kolk, *The Body Keeps the Score*, 210.

and healthy relationships with others. A relationship with a spiritual director can be key in rebuilding emotional capacity and creating growth in healing for the directee. "What I've learned from talking to so many victims of traumatic events, abuse, or neglect is that after absorbing these painful experiences . . . a deep longing to feel needed, validated, and valued begins to take hold."[8] Validating and valuing a directee can be the most important component of the relationship for healing and restoring trust with God and with other human beings.

Conflicting Internal Narratives

A victim of abuse is not often able to create internal narratives or representations of a "safe, consistent caretaker,"[9] and God may be considered one of the unsafe caretakers. If human interaction and experiences create the narrative for a child (and adult) that people are not reliable or trustworthy caregivers, why should God be excluded from being a caregiver, especially when a child is taught that God is our "Father in heaven"? If one's father was not safe, doesn't it make sense that God isn't safe?

In addition to the negative caretaker narrative, many victims of abuse feel that they are responsible for what has happened to them or that they deserved the abuse because they are inherently bad or evil, which ultimately provides an internal framework for explaining *why* people in their world are doing these terrible things and are not good caregivers.

"Most [victims of child abuse] suffer from agonizing shame about the actions they took to survive and maintain a connection with the person who abused them. This was particularly true

---

8. Perry and Winfrey, *What Happened to You?*, 22.
9. Judith Herman, *Trauma and Recovery* (New York, NY: Basic Books, 1997), 107.

if the abuser was someone close to the child, someone the child depended on . . . the result can be confusion about whether one was a victim or a willing participant, which in turn leads to bewilderment about the difference between love and terror; pain and pleasure."[10] If a child felt any sense of pleasure or love during an abusive action, it sets up a dichotomy within the child about who is responsible for the abuse and resulting trauma. A narrative can develop that the child (directee) was inherently responsible for the trauma because it is unfathomable that an adult would choose such actions willingly. "The profound sense of inner badness becomes the core around which the abused child's identity is formed, and it persists into adult life."[11] Shame becomes a core element of self, the mirror in which one sees the self as "I am wrong" as a human being. Shame following childhood sexual abuse can be intensely disempowering, deeply distressing, and potentially destructive to one's sense of self and place in the social and relational world.

This sense of inner evil is compounded by religious teachings that communicate the idea that people are inherently *sinners* and *evil* beings who need God's salvation and cleansing. This fundamental teaching in the Christian faith about a person's sinful nature causes many individuals to confess sins and accept salvation. However, for the traumatized child, if an abusive adult is accusing the victim of leading him/her to do this horrible thing, or that it is the child's fault (*sin*) that it is happening in some shape or form, the victim then has a double sense of inner evil because the belief is that God now also views him or her as the one at fault for the abuse. The sense of inherent evil becomes a no-win situation for the victim and reinforces the authority of the adult to behave in

---

10. Van der Kolk, *The Body Keeps the Score*, 14.
11. Herman, *Trauma and Recovery*, 105.

ways that are traumatic to the child. When perpetrators are attending church or serve in any religious capacity along with the child, "a child cannot understand that people can appear to be good followers of their religion in public and still perpetrate evil, unrighteous acts in private . . . something that hurts this much horrifies and wounds more profoundly than anything the child has ever experienced can only be the product of God's indifference, anger, or malice."[12] Thus, the alignment of pain, suffering, religion, and inherent evil are intertwined through this distorted but understandable framework for trauma in a child's mind.

Directees who are struggling from past sexual abuse are challenged in their very ability to think clearly about who they are at the core. For some, the brain is deceived or trained to believe that there is some core fault within them as a person that causes others to be abusive toward them. This is absolutely essential to understand as a spiritual director, because simply praying a prayer will most likely not be effective in helping an individual understand inherent worth and value. It takes much more time and patience than just a one-off moment or encounter.

Tag, You're It!

One of the unexpected elements of the director-directee relationship is the transference that occurs when the directee is activated by a conversation or memory and then puts the director into the position of rescuer. As directors, we want to be seen as supportive and empowering, yet if we are not careful, the directee can distort these intentions and begin to take out his or her anger and rage on the director. Although we are not providing therapy, this concept is applicable due to the nature of the relationship—

12.   Magrath, *Healing the Ravaged Soul*, 20.

a helping profession—in which one person is more vulnerable than the other. It might even be more poignant in a spiritual direction setting due to the nature of conversation around power, God, dominance, and submission in the Christian living context. Heightened sensitivity to relational dynamics is key for the spiritual director who must maintain a neutral and observant eye on what is happening within the session. Is there transference in play? Has the director replaced the abuser in the victim's mind, and is he or she receiving the backlash of rage? Does the director represent God and the inability to protect the victim from harm? These questions will help guide the director as to what might be going on. Issues of transference need to be addressed gently and carefully with the directee. How do we manage this?

Three Stages of Recovery

According to Herman, we can identify three stages for recovery from trauma: establishing safety, remembrance and mourning, and reconnection with ordinary life.[13] Working with spiritual directees creates a special need for safe places to have conversation, voice doubts or frustrations, and express deep emotions, especially regarding spirituality and God. The role of a director is to ask questions and be curious. Rarely is it to give firsthand advice or knowledge; individuals can find answers to their questions within their own spirit and experience.

Incorporating the three stages of recovery means that establishing safety involves allowing the directee to voice feelings and doubts without any fear of recrimination or reprimand from the director. To create safety means that the director is aware of and educated

---

13. Herman, *Trauma and Recovery*, 155.

on the importance of moving through trauma at the pace of the directee, never forcing memory or recall, and paying attention to the directee's physical and emotional cues during the session as to when to slow down or cease the exploration of memories.

Establishing Safety

For example, when working with a directee who has experienced trauma and is going back to the traumatic event(s), I will be keenly aware of my directee's facial expressions, tone of voice, body language, and verbal expressions. If I sense that the directee has too much to process or that it is becoming unsafe for the directee to continue, we immediately pause and check in about what is happening and how she or he wants to proceed. As already noted earlier, spiritual exploration of an event can bring up deeply buried questions and doubts as to the ability of God to intervene or protect, which can reveal foundational cracks in the person's faith and cause anxiety. At this point, it is critical to step back and assess whether moving forward is positive or detrimental to the healing process. Directees will often say they need to "sit with" what has been said or revealed, and that they need time to absorb the realities of what they just discovered about themselves in relationship to God or childhood teaching about faith. Allowing directees to have space and time to process what a direction session may have brought up is crucial for their need to integrate mind, body, spirit experiences; this might be a long haul. "Controlling when, how much, and which aspect of a traumatic event they share allows a person to create their own therapeutic pattern of recovery."[14] Quick transformation should not be expected and, in fact, can be dangerous or harmful to a directee.

---

14. Perry and Winfrey, *What Happened to You?*, 199.

Remembrance and Mourning

Regarding the second stage of healing, remembrance and mourning, part of the remembrance is to recognize the loss and grief attached to the trauma. "The survivor is called upon to articulate the values and beliefs that she once held and that the trauma destroyed. She stands mute before the emptiness of evil, feeling the insufficiency of any known system of explanation . . . all questions are reduced to one . . . why?"[15] Often, in the face of trauma, a well-meaning person might say "Everything happens for a reason" or provide other placebo answers in the attempt to mitigate the pain. In the wake of trauma, this platitude reinforces the guilt or self-blame of the victim because of the perception that he or she must be part of the reason it happened and must have done something to cause it. Words and phrases can cause incredible damage to a person who is already wrestling with guilt and shame; topping it off with unthoughtful words of reason and logic does little to help move toward healing.

To answer the *why* question, both director and directee must be ready and willing to accept the reality that there may never be a concrete or logical answer. The mystery of *why* or *why me* might remain untenable. If spiritual directors are quick to move to benign phrases for the sake of reducing their own discomfort of not knowing, this can inflict further harm and irreparable damage to the directee. "The question of how a loving God can allow suffering in the world is merely a philosophical exercise. For abuse survivors who have endured horrible trauma, it is a question that is all too personal."[16] In light of this, allowing the directee to ask the hard questions can help facilitate remembrance and mourn-

---

15. Herman, *Trauma and Recovery*, 178.
16. Magrath, *Healing the Ravaged Soul*, 15.

ing, providing space for loss of answers, loss of trust, and loss of belief in the goodness of humanity. These losses, and many others, may lessen in time and become turning points of awareness that help heal, but letting the directee move through this space gives permission to mourn what the directee once thought may have been true but has been proven false over time.

Reconnection with Ordinary Life

The third stage, reconnection with ordinary life, allows a directee to reconstruct the trauma story, transforming it into a new story and a reframed narrative. In relation to spiritual neuroplasticity, if one suffers from insecure attachment from childhood experiences, re-examining God's story through the lens of healthy love and acceptance creates the opportunity to move to a secure means of connecting with God and others. But this is where things get tricky. Even the way we hear, understand, and attempt to enter God's story will be colored by the hues of our own story.[17] Allowing God's narrative to intersect with a trauma narrative is not as easy or straightforward as one might hope. Simply speaking about value, dignity, and worth may not be enough to create a new neural pathway or narrative of hope and self-acceptance. Navigating the integration of God's goodness and love as a trustworthy parent can take years, something that may push a director's limits. This leads us to the conversation about outside therapy and when director roles can get messy or confusing.

In every conversation with a directee who is revisiting trauma, it is essential that spiritual directors do *not* take on the role of a therapist. This is not, in most cases, the place to dive into deep places of dark pain and suffering or mental health issues unless

17.   Curt Thompson, *Anatomy of the Soul* (Carol Stream, IL: Tyndale House, 2010), 138.

the directee brings up the notion of doing so. Even then, it is key that the director has formal training in the area of trauma, to know when and how to keep boundaries within a spiritual setting. Therefore, staying within the bounds of talking about the traumatic event, maybe in general terms without details and how it affects spiritual beliefs, would be the *only* reason to pursue conversation about reconstructing past events with extreme care and sensitivity. *Spiritual direction needs to always complement therapy and does not ever take the place of deep therapeutic work from an experienced, trained therapist.*

Forgiveness Is Mandatory, Right?

Some spiritual directors may want to point their directees toward forgiveness of the perpetrator of abuse in order to help the directee move forward in the healing process. However, Herman provides this word of caution: "Like revenge, the fantasy of forgiveness often becomes a cruel torture, because it remains out of reach for most ordinary human beings . . . true forgiveness cannot be granted until the perpetrator has sought and earned it through confession, repentance, and restitution."[18] Although in Christian teaching forgiveness is essential and key for relationships to flourish between human beings and with God, it is critical to remain neutral in that process until the directee is ready to engage with the process or even talk about it as a concept.

Forgiveness is a delicate process that can recreate a sense of submission for the victim; thus, it is necessary to move slowly through the conversation around this topic and allow for setbacks, anger, pain, and helplessness to emerge as the directee comes to terms with

---

18. Herman, *Trauma and Recovery*, 190.

the reality of what was done to him or her. Directees might say "I'm not ready to forgive. It's too soon and too deep of a wound"; directors must be comfortable living in that space with the directee. Understanding forgiveness from a trauma perspective does not mean we give up on healing efforts for the person to live with interior freedom. Herman supports the idea of restorative love in the directee's life, meaning she or he is able to love others and self, not necessarily the perpetrator, and this allows for moving ahead without needing the perpetrator to ask forgiveness.[19] It is not the same as forgiveness but rather a *disengagement* from the perpetrator.

The idea of not helping a directee forgive may feel disloyal to the Christian belief about the importance of forgiving others, and it may become an area of uncomfortable struggle for the director; however, it could inflict more damage on the directee to force or enforce the teaching of forgiveness in light of abuse, and it is not faithful to the fundamental call of the director to remain curious and alert to what is spoken or unspoken in sessions. It may be that, at some point, the directee feels moved to express words of forgiveness through a spiritual encounter or spiritual practice, but this must come through an intrinsic experience of the Holy. This is not something the director can fabricate for the directee externally, nor should it ever be manipulated.

Attachment

Chapter Three goes into attachment issues in much more detail, but I thought it was worth mentioning here briefly. A directee's personal experience of trauma and unhealthy attachment with a parent can greatly influence understanding or belief in a

19.   Herman, *Trauma and Recovery*, 190.

good and trustworthy God. In fact, a person's perception of God is often reflective of the attachment formed with a parent. This would indicate that the intersection of attachment styles and faith in God is a strong variable in the healing process, for better or worse, and plays a strong role in a spiritually focused conversation, particularly with a childhood sexual abuse (CSA) survivor. Van Hook states, "If we understand a child's sense of spirituality and relationship with God from an attachment theory that God will protect one, abuse to the child disrupts one's spiritual trust and can 'lead to a damaged view and relationship with the divine being.'"[20] So, what do we do with that?

A directee will often be unable to feel God's positive presence due to insecure attachment that developed as a young child. "Our attachment patterns, translated into and through our neural networks, not only affect our relationships with other people, they are one of the primary forces shaping our relationship with God."[21] It is hard to connect with a God who is experienced as distant, judgmental, unpredictable, erratic, or angry when that is what biological parents were like. Separating God from human parentage is nearly impossible, especially when it comes to attachment. Even the most securely attached individual may find it difficult to view God as loving, accepting, positive, or supportive.

Thompson purports that individuals can experience healthy and secure attachment in relationship with God by changing neural networks to reflect what complete attunement *can* look like with our Creator and says that "this is what God seems to be up to—creating good, mysterious things out of messes,"[22] including the mess of trauma and recovery. This is good news and provides

---

20. Van Hook, "Spirituality as a potential resource for coping with trauma," 135

21. Thompson, *Anatomy of the Soul*, 118.

22. Thompson, *Anatomy of the Soul*, 140.

hope for a directee who is struggling in the wake of trauma, yet it can be a long road toward understanding the true nature and character of God due to childhood wounds.

Those who experience disengaged parenting styles, in which parents ignore abusive behavior in the household or with an individual, tend to form anxious and avoidant styles of attachment as adults. Significantly damaging attachment effects occur through the lack of parental response. It is not only what is actively done in parenting/abuse that impacts a child; what is *not done, the lack of protection* is equally or more damaging to a child. Working with directees who experience disengaged parenting as children often transfer that attachment style to God in adulthood, meaning, God didn't care.

The anxious and avoidant styles of relating to others as adults presents a challenge to the director to create a place of engagement and presence to build trust and alliance. Becoming a *protector* of emotions, thoughts, and behavior seems to be a key element in the director-directee relationship. It would be completely understandable for the directee to view God as disengaged or as someone who failed to provide protection, and this could be an area of fragile inquiry if the directee was willing or desirous to discuss this aspect of healing.

Perry and Winfrey underscore the importance of understanding how trauma can adversely affect relationships with not only parents or God but also a director: "Developmental trauma can disrupt our ability to form and maintain relationships . . . there's a high risk that the neural networks involved in reading and responding to other people will be altered."[23] This implies the director must have patience when working with a trauma survivor who ex-

---

23. Perry and Winfrey, *What Happened to You?*, 135.

perienced unhealthy and chaotic interactions with a caregiver. It is important to remember that survivors are not targeting others with difficulty in creating and maintaining a secure relationship, and it is important that directors not take directee comments or distancing as personal attacks. Rather, creating a safe space for cautious intimacy to develop would be ideal and necessary for the directee to feel a sense of connection and relatability with the director to offset any sense of disengagement. To help model secure attachment, directors need to be in a regulated emotional state to help the directee coregulate within a non-threatening environment.

And So?

The bottom line for me as a spiritual director is to recognize that a directee simply having a faith background does not imply immediate or guaranteed positive identification with a God who heals and is restorative. The individual has to come to his or her own conclusion as to the trustworthiness of God and the healing impact of that relationship. Community can play an important role in helping a person feel belonging and connection, and faith can reduce the negative impact of physical and emotional distress post-trauma, yet it appears essential to remain unassuming as to the effect spirituality will have on each person when processing trauma.

Creating a space of safety for a directee requires sensitivity and intention by the director who must pay attention to the person's ability to trust, which hearkens back to attachment issues from childhood. None of this is easy, and it takes effort and concentration for the director to pay attention to these matters. It is exhausting at times and emotionally draining. Yet this is all for the benefit of the person sitting across from us who needs us to be calm, engaged, present, and open to the pain and woundedness of trauma. God forbid that we contribute to further emotional and spiritual damage, intentionally or not. It is on us to make sure that does not happen to the very best of our ability and capacity.

3

The Importance of Attachment

I want to explore the area of attachment patterns in more detail here, because as I have worked with numerous directees, the issue of attachment plays an important role in how one views self, caregivers, others, and God. From infancy our brain is trying to make sense of what the world is offering us in the way of attending to needs on a basic level, or how and why needs are *not* being met, whether those are physical, emotional, or mental. Our neural pathways regarding acceptance, provision, protection, value, and worth are created based on what we experienced as a child with caregivers. As we work with adults who are grappling with unhealthy attachment issues, we must be familiar with basic attachment patterns in order to recognize what might be happening within a directee as they explore their connection with God. We cannot separate our attachment to God from our attachment to those who raised us. Diane Poole Heller, leading expert in attachment theory, discusses unhealthy attachment as "broken connection . . . to our body; broken connection to our sense of self; broken connection to others, especially those we love; broken connection to feeling centered or grounded on the planet; broken connection to God." [24] It is all interconnected.

---

24.   Diane Poole Heller, *The Power of Attachment* (Boulder, CO: Sounds True, 2019), 5.

Perhaps you have heard these words: "How can I trust God? All I know about trust has been distorted and twisted. If God is my 'Father,' then I absolutely will not trust him because my biological father was mean, abusive, and horrible. I did not trust *him* for a second." Words like these, expressed with intense emotion, including rage and hatred, communicate one of the most fundamental and troublesome issues with spirituality and trauma. As stated earlier, often a directee feels unable to experience God's positive or trustworthy presence due to insecure attachment that developed as a young child with one or both parents, resulting in avoidant, anxious (or ambivalent), or disorganized attachment patterns in the adult directee.

In the healing context it is important to revisit the understanding of attachment in the wake of trauma. A key component of spiritual direction is recognizing the *why* behind a directee's difficulty in connecting with a God who is experienced as distant, judgmental, unpredictable, or erratic. One of the challenges in direction is to help the directee untangle the complexity of who God is apart from what was experienced with human caregivers, especially when it comes to attachment. Even the most securely attached individual may find it difficult to view God as loving, accepting, positive, or supportive. "Our attachment patterns, translated into and through our neural networks, not only affect our relationships with other people, they are one of the primary forces shaping our relationship with God."[25] Individuals *can* experience healthy and secure attachment in relationship with God by changing neural networks to reflect what complete attunement can look like with our Creator, but it takes time, sensitivity, knowledge, and patience.

25.   Poole Heller, 118.

Let's take a brief look at attachment styles to better understand some basic principles. As we do so, keep in mind that everyone desires a deep sense of connection and belonging; we are created for relationships. Earlier parenting patterns may have disrupted those longings and created internal barriers or survival mechanisms to protect ourselves from further hurt, but they remain present within each of us as part of our human design. The following paragraphs provide an overview of different attachment and response behaviors and are in no way comprehensive, but they will give a sense of what could be transpiring with a directee during conversations regarding spiritual intimacy.

Secure Attachment

"I felt safe in my home growing up, my parents showed love and respect, and it is not hard for me to see God as one I can trust; I can easily put my faith into my relationships with God and others." Hearing these words, spoken with sincerity and authenticity, lets me know that the directee has probably experienced secure attachment as a child, where value and worth were communicated on an ongoing basis with healthy expressions of love. For someone like this, belief that people are generally good and trustworthy, God included, creates the sense that exploring faith is generally safe and promotes an environment between director and directee that feels relaxed, connected, and engaged. Exploring questions of where God has been present in the directee's life is done with curiosity, flexibility, and an openness to spiritual exercises or practices. Why?

Diane Poole Heller describes secure attachment as *attunement*, where a person feels basic trust in the people around them and in the general environment.[26] Protection and feeling taken care of were daily experiences for children with secure attachment, along with feeling supported and feeling known as an individual. They were around caregivers whom they could depend on for emotional and physical needs being met. A sense of self as a worthy and valuable individual developed as a child; when mistakes were made, the parent lovingly guided them through rough moments. Therefore, connecting with others in adulthood is easily done because interdependence, as well as autonomy, were created throughout life with the idea of needing each other in this world and relying on one another in a trusting manner. Coming back to family feels safe and secure, where being oneself is comfortable and accepted, and basic trust in the goodness of humanity and life is fostered. People with secure attachment generally are more optimistic and can bounce back from difficult situations with resilience and an ability to move forward in life more quickly with positive internal foundations in place.[27]

Directees who have experienced this kind of upbringing, imperfect of course but one which incorporates many of these tenets, are able to openly express their doubts, curiosity, and wonderings about God in current situations. It is not scary for them to seek out connection with their spirituality, and they express a genuine desire to work through narratives that do not make sense or put them at dis-ease. These directees more easily relax into an environment of exploration and feel a sense of trust with their director. The concept of God feels safe to them and foundational to their spirituality; although questions or doubts may arise, searching for more understanding about faith is done within a supportive in-

26. Poole Heller, *The Power of Attachment*, 29–31.
27. Poole Heller, 5.

ternal structure—the directee feels secure in their own self and in their relationship with God. Spiritual directors may be comfortable offering spiritual practices or exercises in these situations, which are accepted through the openness of the directee who has a basic trust in the process.

Avoidant Attachment

"I am fully capable of living life on my own—I don't need anyone else, especially God. No one was there for me as a child or paid attention to me, God included, so why should I expect anyone else to be interested in my life or my pain? I'm told that I need God, but I've been fine without a spiritual life or depending on God for what I need. Faith is all hyped up, in my opinion." The independent, self-sufficient style of relating to others, and God, is called the *dismissive* reaction in adults who experienced avoidant attachment patterns as a child. A person with a dismissive approach to others presents a challenge to the spiritual director for creating a place of engagement and presence to foster trust and alliance with the director.

What exactly is avoidant attachment? The following explanation of the avoidant attachment pattern comes from Diane Poole Heller: "People with this attachment style have a tendency to keep intimacy at arm's length or to diminish the importance of relationships. They often were neglected: left alone too much as children, rejected by their caregivers, or their parents weren't present enough (or only present when teaching them some type of task). Avoidants have disconnected—put the brakes on—their attachment system, so reconnecting to others in safe and healthy ways is extremely important."[28] She goes on to say that avoidant

---

28. Diane Poole Heller, *The Power of Attachment*, 13.

people can feel like outcasts or aliens due to their level of isolation and negative experiences with caregivers. Engaging with others can be risky and extremely uncomfortable because it opens up the possibility of rejection; therefore, keeping to and relying only on oneself is the safest way to navigate life and intimacy. [29] Poole reminds us that looking others in the eye can be disconcerting and scary when childhood memories of eye contact connote anger, disgust, or hatred.[30] Those who did not experience support or connection to others tend to become more left-brained, meaning they are more likely to be logical, factual, and task-focused, as well as demonstrate depleted empathy or emotional warmth due to an underdeveloped right hemisphere.[31] These learned behaviors communicate the message of not needing anyone, perhaps especially God, and present challenges to those with whom they interact on a daily basis. Finally, another piece of dismissive behavior is a lack of comfortability with physical touch, which was likely absent in childhood and could be foreign expression, even including shaking hands, a hug, or a fist bump.

Recognizing a person with dismissive patterns creates unique response and awareness from a spiritual director. Expecting a handshake upon meeting, maintaining eye contact during sessions, or asking what the directee is feeling instead of thinking would not be necessarily helpful in this situation. What needs to happen? Be aware of building a relationship through consistent caring, support, and engagement, and do not become discouraged if a bond is not created in the first few sessions, if indeed at all. I met with someone for two years and never felt a deep sense of heart connection with this individual. Conversations were cere-

---

29.   Poole Heller, 62.
30.   Poole Heller, 65.
31.   Poole Heller, 70.

bral, not emotive, and although these sessions were rich and provided moments of deep insight, I did not feel she bonded with me emotionally, and that was fine. I understood that she was doing the best she could, given her trauma, and we had a good working relationship, just without the warm connection that is sometimes felt with a directee. She stated she felt my empathy and that was good enough.

It can be tempting to take rejection personally if one does not feel any sort of connection with a directee who experiences avoidant attachment. Yet understanding the lack of interaction or caring the directee may have experienced as a child, resulting in the need to become self-sufficient in many ways, can remind the director to become a *protector* of emotions, thoughts, and behavior, to be fully present emotionally and mentally. Role modeling healthy attention and acceptance, having kind eyes, and respecting personal space can promote safety, trust, and alliance for the directee. (This also means being aware of transference, meaning the directee begins to project feelings of anger onto you as the director, and holding appropriate boundaries to protect both parties.) Recognizing an avoidant attachment style also aids in understanding why the directee may view God as disinterested or neglectful, which would be an area of fragile inquiry in the session, needing to be handled with gentleness and curiosity, avoiding the pitfall of using Bible verses or cliches that might be unhelpful at this point.

Ambivalent Attachment

"I never knew if Mom would be there for me or if she would be preoccupied with other things when I wanted to connect with her. Sometimes she was all 'ears' and sometimes she told me to leave her alone. It was so unpredictable, so I walked on tenter-hooks around her." When I hear words to this effect, I immediately know that there might be some anxious or ambivalent attachment issues at play. What does this mean? Diane Poole Heller states: "People with the ambivalence adaptation deal with a lot of anxiety about having their needs met or feeling secure in being loved or lovable. Their parent might have shown them love, but as children they never knew when their parents might get distracted and utterly pull the rug out from underneath them. Their care was unpredictable or notably intermittent."[32] She explains that people with an anxious response to others as an adult can look needy or clingy, because they get worried when a loved one leaves for work or does not respond immediately to a phone call or text.[33] There is a pervasive feeling of uncertainty about the relationship and whether it is solid or not, due to a parent exhibiting both presence and abandonment. Focusing on others, relationships, and emotions becomes detrimental to work completion, tasks, normal functions of daily living, and they find regulation of emotions through others' actions and responses.[34] Someone with ambivalent attachment does not have confidence in a sense of self but relies on those around them for connection or validation, resulting in overdependence on external cues. Reassurance is important for the directee, who is waiting for the bottom to drop out at any moment.[35]

Talking with a directee who has not experienced intimate relationships as consistent or predictable will not be comfortable with the idea of a God who is "always there for us" or who "supplies

---

32.   Poole Heller, *The Power of Attachment*, 14.
33.   Poole Heller, 86.
34.   Poole Heller, 87.
35.   Poole Heller, 95.

all our needs," and may not believe that we will be there for them as directors. This type of assuring verbiage causes anxiety because it is something they have not experienced, and it may feel fake or disingenuous. We must be careful not to assume a directee's readiness for a statement we might want to make about God being available 24/7; being aware of our language can help build the bridge of understanding as we listen and reflect the directee's experience. "Consistency and reassurance are paramount,"[36] so we must realize that even the small things, such as communicating about appointment changes or availability, are important for creating a sense of constancy. Exploring what the directee imagines a relationship to look like with a consistent parent and what that would feel like in the imagination might be a place to start in helping them find a mind/body connection with what is truly desired deep in the soul, and then slowly explore what that could look like for them spiritually.

Disorganized Attachment

"There were times when I desperately wanted my caregiver to hold me when I was scared or nervous, but I couldn't ask them to do that because they were the one who hurt me; it was so confusing and crazy-making." When a directee expresses this type of statement, you may be encountering someone with disorganized attachment patterns, which are extremely complex, encompassing both avoidant and ambivalent patterns but with much more fear of the parent. They are unsure of their own feelings and do not feel a sense of safety within themselves or from others, and they are in survival mode most of the time. "They often suffer

---

36. Poole Heller, 14.

from psychological and physical confusion . . . disorganized folks are often emotionally dysregulated, dealing with sudden shifts in arousal, or dissociated and checked out."[37] The brain is wired to deal with threat at all times, creating a false interpretation of a safe situation, making it difficult to connect with others and feel secure in any relationship. Internal conflict reigns supreme with two forces warring against each other: the instinct for connection and the instinct for survival.[38] A "freeze" response is common for those with disorganized attachment, meaning the body is unable to move even though the mind wants to go forward—it's a state of feeling stuck.[39] The sympathetic nervous system—our threat and fear detection system—is usually working overtime. This will be explained a bit further in the chapter.

Working with a directee who has experienced fear from the person who was supposed to protect them requires the director to be hypervigilant in reading body language, especially if the freeze response occurs. It may look as if the directee is being passive, but it is imperative to understand the internal war raging between running and staying. Disorganized attachment also brings up many questions, doubts, and skepticism about faith in the character of God; is God safe, should I fear God, did God punish or cause hurt in my life? Saying that trauma "happened for a reason" communicates to a trauma survivor that protection from God should not be expected because there was a "higher purpose" within the trauma. This is not only damaging but creates further confusion and fear within the directee about God's character, for a directee cannot move toward a Being who has inflicted or sanctioned harm.

---

37.   Poole Heller, *The Power of Attachment*, 14.
38.   Poole Heller, 125.
39.   Poole Heller, 126.

As a director, staying regulated in the session at all times can help the directee feel safe in the room and with you. Remaining calm and in a listening state demonstrates that you are present, providing space for them to explore the fear and confusion they have toward others and God. As much as we want to immediately help build a bridge to God's love and acceptance, we need to avoid spouting any clichés or glib answers that create a climate of distrust or shame for the directee. The work toward creating an environment of healing requires patience and unconditional acceptance from the director to maintain a regulated state of mind and an open posture for the directee to explore who God is at their own pace.

Disengaged Attachment

"When I was being abused, my other parent ignored the situation, or didn't want to get involved. It was like I was invisible even though I was right there in front of the other adult in the room while being beaten. She didn't stop anything or step in to help. I was totally on my own." A study done by attachment researchers on how disengaged parenting—meaning the parent did not intervene or pay attention to a child in need—found that those who experienced disengaged parenting styles and had experienced abuse formed anxious and avoidant styles of attachment as adults and were found to have significantly damaged attachment effects through the lack of parental response.[40] Therefore, it is not only what is *actively* done in parenting that impacts a child, but it is also what is *not* done that is equally or more damaging to the

40.   Briere et al., *Child Abuse and Neglect*, 67, 260–70

child. The lack of a protector is significant in forming unhealthy attachments as older adults.

Directees who consistently say things regarding God's absence or lack of protecting them might be voicing the disengaged attachment style, and this is a very real sensory experience of feeling alone during traumatic moments in their lives. Putting forth the assurances that God was in fact with them in those moments does not create stability or relief for many directees; it feels insincere, dismissive, or like a flat out lie. Staying present, engaged, and assuring the directee of being seen and heard is a key factor in this type of relationship. Over time, and if it feels appropriate after validating the directee's experience, directing a person to a Psalm that expresses abandonment, pain, and isolation *might* be a starting point of reconnecting with others who historically felt the same way. However, this could be further damaging, so it must be navigated carefully and with the directee's permission.

Attachment and the Director

Perry and Winfrey underscore the importance of understanding how trauma can adversely affect relationships not only with parents or God but also with a person of a helping profession: "Developmental trauma can disrupt our ability to form and maintain relationship. . . . There's a high risk that the neural networks involved in reading and responding to other people will be altered."[41] This implies the director must have patience when working with a trauma survivor who may have experienced unhealthy and chaotic interactions with a caregiver. It is important to remember that survivors are not targeting others with difficulty

41.   Perry and Winfrey, *What Happened To You?*, 135.

in creating and maintaining a secure relationship, and it is important to not take comments or distancing from directees as personal attacks. Rather, creating a safe space for cautious intimacy to develop would be ideal and necessary for the directee to feel a sense of connection and relatability with the director. "Regulation is the key to creating a safe connection."[42] To do this as directors we need to be in a regulated emotional state to help the directee co-regulate and feel he/she is in a nonthreatening environment. Co-regulation means staying calm, nonanxious, and attentive.

Spiritual directors need to be aware of strong, childhood narratives that play an important role in a directee's story, but also that the relational aspect of being a positive spiritual resource can help *rewrite* the narrative for spiritual healing and the possibility of secure attachment with God in the future. There is hope, although it is not an immediate or a quick fix, and we can never rush healing.

Neuroscience and Attachment

Our brains and bodies are amazingly complex, and we are constantly evaluating input from external and internal sources. Even before birth, our neural networks of safety were being formed as we experienced connection, fear, anxiety, security, love, and acceptance from our mother. As soon as we entered the world, our body and brain were scanning the environment for clues and cues as to who would take care of us, supply our needs, and offer comfort. Whether these things happened or not affected our basic understanding of life, the external world, and our internal world.

---

42. Perry and Winfrey, *What Happened To You?*, 144.

Parasympathetic Nervous System

Our stress response to what was going on around us created neural circuits that informed our body and mind as to what was considered safe or dangerous. If we were taken care of, provided for, comforted and attended to, cuddled, and received messages of love and value as a child, we probably experienced secure attachment in some form and our *parasympathetic nervous system* told us all was well; this state of being means we could relax and enjoy our surroundings, our blood flow was primarily going to our prefrontal cortex, the place in the brain where we think, problem solve, make decisions and live into an optimistic sense of well-being. We could rest and digest, so to speak, and allow ourselves to be in relative peace with ourselves and others.

Sympathetic Nervous System

However, if we experienced lack of needs being met, emotional abuse, harsh words, physical harm; witnessed violence, lived in chaotic environments, or felt shame at our core just for being alive, we developed a heightened sense of fear, danger, and threat. Our *sympathetic nervous system* was highly activated, which means our body is ready to fight, flee, freeze, or collapse at any time for survival. We might struggle to focus or problem solve from the prefrontal cortex because it has been shut down; all our body's energy and blood flow is going to our muscles to run, fight, remain still, or enter into a submissive state of collapse. The world is perceived as dangerous and threatening, and we are most often in a state of threat detection as our radar for harm is constantly scanning our environment. If this is the case, we most likely experienced avoidant, ambivalent, disorganized, or disengaged attach-ment from our parents or caregiver.

Stress Response and Spirituality

Why is this stress response in our body important to know about in ourselves and others? We are unconsciously conditioned to see the world through our body's state of being; either we are generally relaxed and able to handle adversity with resilience and flexibility, or we are constantly on the lookout for danger and our body is tense most of the time. We are largely unaware of our natural state of response because it is so deeply ingrained within us, similar to being unaware of attachment issues that are buried deep in our psyche. We have a neuropsychobiological response in daily life that determines our behaviors and interactions from a place deep within ourselves, and we are largely unaware of the impact it has upon us.

My few words here do not do justice to the complexity of neuroscience, but as spiritual directors we must be somewhat fa-miliar with the body's stress response as we work with directees. We can recognize nuances of heightened states of threat awareness and detection (the sympathetic state), and we can recognize some-one in a state of parasympathetic response (rest and digest state). Watching for cues of safety—relaxed, calm, engaged—can let us know how to interact with a directee. Sensing cues of threat or danger—hands twisting, nervous posture, sudden reactions, eye gaze aversion, looking for an escape route, legs bouncing, change of voice tone—can alert us to a person's sense of feeling unsafe, and we must respond with gentleness, curiosity, and awareness of our own body response.

Our body, mind, and spirit are intimately connected, so when one feels out of whack, so do the others. It is possible to retrain our body and mind to operate generally from a parasympathetic state of being, but this requires much time and attention from doctors, therapists, psychologists, support systems, and spiritual directors. For the purpose of this handbook, I want to acknowledge the power of neural pathways and how these inform our mind and body of safety or danger. Growing up in a household where one did not feel safe at one level or many levels most likely created a heightened sympathetic nervous system response, and this is important to recognize as it affects all areas of life. If our body did not feel safe, nothing felt safe.

As spiritual directors, being aware of neural pathways and stress response systems enables us to be sensitive and supportive of those who struggle to make sense of spirituality and God in a dangerous world. "Feeling someone or something is there to keep you safe while your views of reality shift allows your mind to be less fearful in the moment. It lets you open up to new and disorienting states precisely because you feel secure."[43] We can help engage the parasympathetic nervous system in our sessions just by our attention to details and noticing what is occurring in the room, and offering to breathe calmly and deeply with our directee to foster a more regulated system.

Brain, Belief, and Behavior

Neuroscience research has uncovered some fascinating concepts regarding faith and the impact on the brain. One of those discoveries is in relation to one part of the brain that alerts us to

---

43.   David DeSteno, *How God Works* (New York: Simon & Schuster, 2021), 98.

danger, the anterior cingulate cortex (ACC), which also involves learning, emotional regulation, memory, moral behavior, conflict monitoring, and much more.[44] When activated through sensing a threat or making an error in judgment, patterns similar to those of anxiety disorders emerge and intensify within the ACC and amygdala (our threat detection center). What is fascinating about this is that research on those who had faith or a strong, positive belief in God exhibited *less* activity in the ACC when confronted with making a poor decision or experiencing emotional dysregulation. In other words, less stress.[45] DeSanto makes the point that there are different neurological responses measured by scientific tests that show a difference in how the brain processes threats or failure when faith or positive spiritual belief is involved.[46]

Why does this matter? For me, it provides hope that as we work with directees and help them move toward healing faith, new neural pathways and responses are being developed that can aid in alleviating the stress response system, and instead increase trust in the world around them. Newberg and Waldman state, "If you contemplate God long enough, something surprising happens in the brain. Neural functioning begins to change. Different circuits become activated, while others become deactivated."[47] New beliefs about who we are, the possibility of secure attachment, and hope in the future are a *real possibility* through our work with directees.

Another exciting discovery regarding the ACC involves our interpersonal relationships and our ability to feel compassion and

44. Andrew Newberg and Mark Waldman, *How God Changes Your Brain* (New York: Ballantine Books, 2009), 42.
45. DeSteno, *How God Works*, 17.
46. DeSteno, *How God Works, 17.*
47. Newberg and Waldman, *How God Changes Your Brain*, 1.

empathy toward others. When focusing and meditating on God's love, the ACC becomes activated and the neurological circuits that help us feel compassion toward others are strengthened.[48] It appears that faith and being able to meditate on God's love also play a huge part in how the brain gets wired, or can be rewired!

On the flip side, when someone experiences fear through religious teaching, activity increases in the amygdala (the fear and threat detection center), creating high anxiety and aggression toward others. When the amygdala senses something is amiss externally and is presenting danger, the sympathetic nervous system is aroused and the ACC functions of compassion and empathy are inhibited; the seat of reasoning and problem-solving, the prefrontal cortex, is also shut down.[49] Ongoing fear affects the brain by shutting down compassion and empathy for others, which in itself is sobering.

What this means for me is that parts of the brain are impacted by what we believe to be true about God, which impacts our interpersonal connections with others. It makes sense why some of our directees really struggle to accept love when all they have known is fear. The challenges presented by directees about belief in who God is based on childhood experiences, whether positive or negative, makes sense in how these beliefs impact behavior toward self and others. In a nutshell, fear in any capacity, but especially when connected to spirituality, breeds intolerance and the damaged ability to feel compassion for others, while beliefs that foster God's love activate positive interactions and increased acceptance of those who might have different beliefs or viewpoints. If we can grasp how deep this concept is at a neurological level, we

48. Newberg and Waldman, *How God Changes Your Brain*, 53.
49. Newberg and Waldman, 53.

can have compassion and love toward directees who are struggling to feel or accept love from God and who are living from a basic sense of fear through trauma.

Brain science is confirming that belief influences behavior at a neurological level, and this creates hope, because new neural pathways are possible. "The anterior cingulate . . . integrates the activity of different parts of the brain in a way that allows self-consciousness to emerge, especially as it applies to how we see ourselves in relation to the world."[50] If we can help directees begin to experience compassion toward themselves, toward others, and toward God, we can be part of a healing journey that fosters wholeness, authenticity, secure attachment, and trust. We are part of interpersonal connection when new neural pathways develop through a positive and safe relationship with a directee, and something bigger is happening as the brain changes. Such knowledge can be a hopeful starting point for spiritual sojourners. Trauma has the effect of creating a constant sense of danger or hypervigilance to threat, and our gentle responses as spiritual directors to those who have experienced trauma can help begin fostering new pathways that engage the ACC and compassion, empathy, and acceptance for themselves and for what may have happened to them.

As stated before, the journey is slow, painful, arduous, and vulnerable, and spiritual directors must be open to cautious exploration with the hope that a person may indeed see themselves in a new light, as worthwhile and valuable. Basic knowledge of how the brain works and responds to trauma enables the director to see beyond the behavior and beliefs, approaching a directee with increased sensitivity and patience, value, and hope.

---

50. Newberg and Waldman, 124.

4

Doing Our Personal Best

Research conducted for this handbook has elucidated several best practices in spiritual direction that would be considered essential for spiritual directors who are working with trauma survivors. As stated before, these are delicate, sensitive situations that need intentionality behind conversation as well as boundaries in the direction session. It cannot be overstated that those who have trauma of this kind in their background have emotional wounds that go deep into the soul. Spiritual directors must be aware of the damage that could be further inflicted within a session if acute intention is missing from the director. The following practices have been gleaned from articles and books that have specifically looked at spirituality and trauma in some form or fashion.

Knowing Personal Limitations

The primary best practice I have discovered is knowing one's own limitations for empathy or compassion as a spiritual director with someone who struggles with conceptualizing God as a loving or protecting Being. The director may personally feel deep love from God and have a strong sense of healthy spirituality, but this does not allow or give permission for any projection of these feelings or thoughts onto the directee. Respecting the boundaries and experiences of the directee is one of the fundamental principles of the therapeutic setting.

Let me outline several expectations of a spiritual director that need self-examination as to where we are with these expectations:

> [First, the] sole purpose is to promote the recovery of the [directee], which means bringing all the skills and knowledge available to the session for the sake of the [directee's healing]; second, power is implicit in the relationship, so the use of power given to the [director by directee] is only for healing and never for inflicting further damage; third, the [director] does not advocate anything that would be of self-interest, nor does the [director] take sides in any [directee's] internal conflict or struggle but instead stays neutral.[51]

These directives remind the director of the centrality of focus on the directee and provide restraint for the director to impose or enforce any image of God/parent identity onto an individual. These parameters create room for the directee to explore, discover, acknowledge, or verbalize what is being connected between an adult abuser and the image of God. Giving directees control of the conversation is key in providing a safe environment in which spiritual direction can take place.

Building Trust

Spiritual directors need to incorporate the best practice of building trust with the directee and not assume it is automatically present. As directors, we can often assume that trust will be part of the relationship from the very beginning; however, that would be a faulty assumption and a dangerous one, possibly setting up a failed relationship with the directee. Lack of trust with persons

---

51. Herman, *Trauma and Recovery*, 35.

in an authoritative role is a common result when trauma is part of a person's story. Directors will need to slowly build trust through sensitive dialogue, respect, reading emotional cues, and creating safety for the directee to simply exist in the session without any expectation. Trust is foundational to any relationship, requiring intentional effort and patience when working with trauma survivors. A gentle tone of voice, slow movements, paying attention to body language and verbal language, and concise communication are just a few ideas of how to interact with directees who might find it difficult to engage with a person in a role that might be interpreted as one of spiritual authority rather than companionship.

Trust is also built when the spiritual director does not take negative comments or negative behavior personally but is able to incorporate such actions or words as part of the trust-building process. As directors, we want to be seen as supportive and empowering. However, if we are not careful, the directee can distort these intentions and begin to take out anger and rage on the director. To promote emotional and healing connection with a directee, it is essential to create a relationship of trust through attunement to the directee's body response to triggering words or phrases. Being aware of what words or behaviors upset or alter the directee's feeling of safety is key to recognizing when an internal shift happens within the directee, who might then focus anger or frustration on the director. Heightened sensitivity to relational dynamics is key for the spiritual director who must maintain a neutral and observant eye to what is happening within the session. Again, realizing this is not a personal attack will help the spiritual director to maintain a sense of acceptance and the ability to hold space for the emotional response.

Language Is Key

Another best practice is to be keenly aware of language used in sessions with a directee. Because spirituality is the main focus in seeking out a spiritual director, the concept of God is going to emerge in conversation and become an area of interest and exploration. Many survivors "struggle daily with deep theological questions about a suffering humanity and the nature of God"[52] and often stop attending church as adults because it is too strange and discordant to be inside a church building due to shame and internal discomfort. In line with this awkwardness, it can be too easy for the spiritual director to forget discretion about terms used regarding God as Father/Mother or Protector when alluding to a spiritual principle or image. Taking a moment to stop and think about what is being said is critical in creating trust and safety for the directee. Asking what term is acceptable to the directee when conversing about God is key in the initial conversations to establish protocol and parameters for verbiage in relation to spiritual concepts. For example, does the directee want to use the word *parent, higher being, God,* or *Jesus*? Is there another word that is preferable? I was once talking with a directee who shuddered when God was alluded to as a male, and she could not continue the conversation. Recognizing my mistake, I asked if she could think of God in female terms? She said yes and visibly relaxed as she recalled the positive relationship she had with her mother. Simply asking the question communicates sensitivity and desire to create a safe environment for the directee and can help establish trust in the early stages of a relationship.

---

52. Magrath, *Healing the Ravaged Soul,* 15.

In church, songs and lyrics can evoke traumatic memories or elicit a visceral response that suggest power, surrender, dominance, or denying of self. The song itself may have a positive message overall, but to a victim of abuse, specifically sexual abuse, the words can recreate moments of terror, isolation, helplessness, entrapment, fear, and anger, and be overwhelming. Sometimes the actual physical feeling of a trauma can be experienced just through the mention of a word.[53] Scripture passages can also have the same effect, causing distress within a victim who may be feeling the weight of words carrying authoritative and constrictive messages from an angry and controlling God, reflecting the character of a biological father. Very little thought is given in the wider church venue to those who might experience a negative reaction to such lyrics or language, but it is critical in the one-to-one setting that knowledge, awareness, and experience guide the director's sense of appropriate verbiage regarding spirituality to reduce harm.

Raising community awareness of how vocabulary in songs or preaching can recreate trauma for abuse survivors is also a best practice for spiritual directors. The community is usually part of the healing process and requires education on how to be contributors of restoration when encountering trauma history. One of the ways this can happen is through language sensitivity around spirituality, and respectfully deferring to the preferred term a survivor has for any higher power. This may be uncomfortable or may challenge doctrinal teachings for individuals, but this is where the immediate community for a victim can support and underscore the importance of using language that is tolerable and acceptable for one who has been traumatized. Rebuilding a person's life through communal interaction should be enough to stir conscious aware-

---

53. Magrath, *Healing the Ravaged Soul*, 11.

ness of how we speak to those around us who need our attention to words and images for the sake of healing and restoration. In the words of Herman, "Assurances of safety and protection are of the greatest importance."[54] This is our mandate as community members and best practice of spiritual directors.

Emotional Development and Attachment

Another best practice is to be aware that a trauma survivor is most likely stuck in an emotional and mental stage of development correlating with the age of trauma onset. The age of an adult who is in spiritual direction does not necessarily determine the emotional maturity of the individual, who may be frozen at a much earlier age. I had a directee who was a grown woman but seemed stuck in her emotional age at around 6 or 7 due to the abuse she suffered as a young girl. Understanding the concept of trauma thwarting development in some areas helped me attune to this possibility, which enabled me to support her as she coached her young self into a healthier state of being and self-acceptance.

Attachment issues might be a key factor for the directee in the ability to move forward in mental and emotional maturity. Experiencing anxious, ambivalent, or disorganized attachment creates the possibility that attachment with God is reflective of the attachment with a parent. Best practice would be to understand attachment styles at a deep level to help broaden awareness of what could be happening with a directee who has experienced trauma.

This is not a comprehensive analysis of how to handle emotional and attachment conflicts, so my encouragement is to study

---

54. Herman, *Trauma and Recovery*, 61.

more on your own and get a good handle on attachment theory. Issues of attachment are complex and often addressed with a therapist in depth, but I feel it is worth mentioning here simply as a point of acknowledgment. Our human mind is incredibly and uniquely wired; we can never completely understand or fathom what might be going on in the person sitting across from us. However, I believe it is the responsibility of the director to become acquainted with attachment styles for personal and professional development and to be cognizant of why trust in God might be so difficult and challenging.

Respecting Spiritual Boundaries and Maintaining Neutrality

The research is clear that people can indeed find healing through spirituality but only when the spiritual director gives space and freedom for the directee to express beliefs about God and how spirituality has been impactful, either positively or negatively. Safety in exploring how faith affects trauma and vice versa is key for an individual to have beliefs held with respect and value, especially if these are different from the director's beliefs and values. Holding sacred space for a person to be vulnerable in vocalizing what has been challenging or damaging in the wake of abuse is vital to the emotional safety of the directee. In no way is it acceptable for a spiritual director to invalidate or refute a person's experience of God; this is a violation of a direction session and crosses ethical boundaries.

Spiritual healing becomes part of the process only when a spiritual director is able to hold, with respect and dignity, another's viewpoint or belief in spiritual matters and maintain neutrality. This requires curiosity and genuine listening by the director to truly hear and value what is being said, putting aside personal values and beliefs. It can be difficult to hold one's values in check when someone is expressing something that is in opposition to what we believe, yet this is one way to minimize further damage to the person who is looking for spiritual healing.

Moving at the Directee's Pace

It is not good practice to push a conversation forward or ask for too much, too soon. As spiritual directors, we must give space and time to the directee and allow him or her to discuss or disclose whatever is comfortable. We cannot intrude or force conversation in any shape or form, especially when it comes to matters of trauma and abuse. Being extremely careful and attentive to the pace of the conversation and allowing the directee to be in control of that pace enables a sense of empowerment. It is often critical to step back and assess whether moving forward is positive or detrimental to the healing process. Knowing when to refer to a therapist is critical in the spiritual direction conversation; the best-case scenario is working with a directee who is already seeing a therapist.

Asking permission of the directee is key when using lectio divina, holy imagination, inviting them into a biblical narrative, or any other spiritual exercise, because this allows them the power to have choice and to feel control in the session. When someone has experienced trauma, that sense of empowerment is essential for healing. In this handbook I intentionally do not give specific or blanket exercises to use in sessions regarding trauma because those are always unique to the situation, but asking permission before any exercise or practice should be a given in each session to give the directee agency.

Self-Compassion as a Director

The element of compassion for oneself as a spiritual director is also a best practice. We can become dysregulated by the stories we hear from our directees; we can be internally triggered by a response from the directee, or by emotions that arise as we feel anger, outrage, or frustration about what we are hearing. These situations can easily change our facial expression, tone of voice, posture, or other nonverbal reactions, which are picked up on by the directee, who may feel she or he has said or done something wrong. It is essential to be transparent in that moment and let the other know that we have been triggered or dysregulated and need a minute to recenter and regroup. Perhaps holding your own hand or shifting postures to regain a sense of presence for the directee might be one way to recenter yourself. By naming discomfort or strong emotion, we can assure the directee that we were thrown off for a minute, but now we are back in the room and present. By doing this, we can help any minor rupture or misunderstanding in the conversation be quickly repaired and identified for ongoing trust to develop.

Having someone we can talk to without violating confidentiality is also important for spiritual directors. Similar to therapists, we can carry many burdens on our shoulders and feel the effects of weighty matters from the stories we encounter. Meeting with a spiritual director ourselves, meditation, or other avenues of self-care are essential to staying healthy in any helping profession, including spiritual direction. Weekly, monthly, or yearly reflection points are invaluable in helping discern where we have missed the mark or have improved in areas of working with survivors. Continued learning is one of the most important ways we can move forward in self-development for the sake of our directees. And it goes without saying that our own relationship with God remains the center and focus of our attention. We cannot give to others what we do not have within our soul to impart, so keeping a rhythm of life for growth and restoration is key.

Finally: Play. Laugh. Enjoy those whom you love. And find well-being every day. May we find the healing within our own lives that we seek for others and be instruments of peace and wholeness.

Resources

Amthor, Frank. *Neuroscience for Dummies.* Mississauga, Ontario: John Wiley & Sons, Inc., 2016.

Baugh, Ken. *Unhindered Abundance.* Colorado Springs, Colorado: NavPress, 2021.

Bayne, H., and M. Tylsova. "Understanding and incorporating God representations within counseling." *Counseling and Values* 64, no. 2 (2019): 148-67.

Beck, J. "Self and soul: Exploring the boundary between psychotherapy and spiritual formation." *Journal of Psychology and Theology,* 31, no. 1 (2003): 24-36.

Borelli, J., K. Ensink, L. Normandin, and M. Target. "Childhood abuse and attachment insecurity: Associations with child psychological difficulties." *American Journal of Orthopsychiatry* 20, no. 1 (2020): 115-24.

Briere, J., M. Runtz, , E. Eadie, N. Bigras, and N. Godbout. "Disengaged parenting: Structural equation modeling with child abuse, insecure attachment, and adult symptomatology." *Child Abuse & Neglect* 67 (2017): 260-70.

Capaldo, M., and R. Perrella. "Child maltreatment: An attachment theory perspective." *Mediterranean Journal of Clinical Psychology* 6, no. 1 (2018).

Dana, Deb. Compassion in Therapy Summit. April 25, 2022.
https://www.compassionintherapy.com/stream/polyvagal-
theory-for-therapist-self-regulation/.

Gaskin-Wasson, Ashley L, Kristin L. Walker, Lilian J. Shin, and
Nadine J. Kaslow. "Spiritual well-being and psychological ad-
justment: Mediated by interpersonal needs?" *Religious Health*
57 (2018): 1376–91. https://doi.org/10.1007/s10943-016-
0275-y.

Ganz, Zev. "God as self-object and therapeutic potential of divine
failure." *Clinical Social Work Journal* 45, no. 4 (December
2017): 332-43. https://doi.org/10.1007/s10615-016-0608-z.

Guyon, R., M. Fernet, and N. Godbout. "'A journey back to my
wholeness': A qualitative metasynthesis on the relational
and sexual recovery process of child sexual abuse survivors."
International Journal of Child and Adolescent Resilience 7, no. 1
(2020): 72-86. https://doi.org/10.7202/1072589.

Herman, Judith. *Trauma and Recovery.* New York: Basic Books,
1997.

MacGinley. M., J. Breckenridge, and J. Mowll. "A scoping review of
adult survivors' experiences of shame following sexual abuse
in childhood." *Health and Social Care in the Community.* (May
1, 2019). DOI: 10.1111/hsc.12771.

Magrath, Sue. *Healing the Ravaged Soul.* Eugene, OR: Cascade
Books, 2016.

Newberg, Andrew, and Mark Robert Waldman. *How God Changes
Your Brain.* New York: Ballantine Books, 2010.

Perry, Bruce D., and Oprah Winfrey. *What Happened to You?* New
York: Flatiron Books, 2021.

Thompson, Curt. *Anatomy of the Soul.* Carol Stream, IL: Tyndale House, 2010.

Van der Kolk, Bessel A. *The Body Keeps the Score.* New York: Penguin Books, 2014.

Van Hook, Mary Patricia. "Spirituality as a potential resource for coping with trauma." *Social Work & Christianity*, 43, no. 1 (Spring 2016): 7-25.

SCAN HERE to learn more about Invite Press, a premier publishing imprint created to invite people to a deeper faith and living relationship with Jesus Christ.

Printed in the USA
CPSIA information can be obtained
at www.ICGtesting.com
LVHW061112181223
766705LV00057B/3377

9 781953 495792